Patterns
of
Life

✼

Lee Kane

Contents

❦

Contents

Athletics

THE RACE OF LIFE

An oval track you run around,
To try and win a race;
Run your opponent into the ground,
At a steady striding pace.

Not everyone can be a winner,
No matter how hard they try;
From the time they're a beginner,
Until the day they die.

As long as the effort's there,
And one strives for their best;
It's not that uncommon or rare,
To meet a challenged test.

Regardless of where in the pack,
Never stop and look back;
Strive to be the best you can,
Don't be known as an also ran.

ACTIVITIES DIRECTOR

The Activities Director is also known as the A.D.
Schedules building use, Arts/Sports for the community to see.
Many people attend football games in the stand.
Have applauded our Outstanding Marching Band.
As they play the school fight song.
Exemplifying what it is to belong.
Many duties are done behind the scene.
To serve the young population teen.
There's meetings. Schedules and Reports.
To also cover the varied sports.
And when fans attend any school event.
Sportsmanship is the Number One Intent.
So when those viewers attend.
It's our school's best response we send.
The excellent staff spends many hours.
Displaying for you their dutied powers.
The A.D. has to be fair in his approach.
To properly evaluate each coach.
The physical work is done by his crew.
All being trained for what they do.
His skills have to be most prudent.
As he provides for each H.S. student.
He also addresses each complaint.
Knowing everyone is not a saint.
The final result is one of care.
That is why he is always there.

CROSS COUNTRY

For Cross Country, you run, run, run,
To compete with others and have fun.

Should be fast at the start,
To get near the lead;
Do it with best of heart,
Set your pace to never cede.

On Flatlands, Lowlands, or the Hills,
Run at a prolonged steady pace;
Hopefully, there'll be many thrills,
As you complete each contested race.

Run the course all the way,
Try and claim first place,
Work hard, maybe someday,
You break the tape, and your face.

Will glow with a broad mouth smile,
To show you worked and were the best,
Making all those workouts worthwhile,
As you proudly/valiantly met the test.

Win or lose always try,
To improve yourself and time,
Never let a race go by,
That didn't max to your prime.

Compete for yourself and your team,
To claim a victory at each meet.
If you're all on the focused beam,
Getting that medal/trophy will be so sweet.

BASEBALL — SOFTBALL

Baseball — Softball — Oh So Round,
Hit them in the air and on the ground;
Sometimes you never hit them at all,
'Specially if the bat misses the ball.

You Hit and Run, Occasionally Steal,
To keep your opponents on their heel;
Step # 1 — Get to First Base.
Step # 2 — Get safely there to make your case.
Step # 3 — Get to Third/Listen for the coach's word.
Step # 4 — Cross the plate, don't be late.

In the field when the ball's alive,
Throw out your opponent before they arrive,
On the ground or in the air,
Make sure the ball is the first thing there.

Play the game you so dearly love,
With needed equipment and proper glove.
Hear the announcer call your name,
As you play out each exiting game.

Give your all with heart and soul,
Should always be your gamely goal.
A determined will, a vow so solemn,
You'll succeed in the Victory column.

PING PONG

There's a sporting game called Ping Pong.
You can play it right, or play it wrong.
You use a paddle, You use a ball.
As you try to encompass it all.
Be sure and master your serve.
To test your opponent and their nerve.
Its pace can be a fast moving game.
Results won't always be the same.
A contested volley lands over the net.
Hopefully a point you will get.
Backhand - Forehand a clean return.
Successful action for you to earn.
Overhead - Sideways, eventually a slam.
Will let you know who I am.

BASKETBALL

A Big Round Ball put it in the Hole,
Rebound, Pick, Screen and Roll,
Do Your Part in Playing a Role,
To Help Your Team Attain a Goal.

Dribble and Shoot, Ripple the Cord,
As you light up the Scoreboard,
Score more Points than Your Foe,
Perpetual Motion on the Go.

Play Zone Defense — or Man-to-Man,
Better yet — Press when you can,
Motion Offense — Run the Flex,
Female or Male — Regardless of Sex.

A Basket Scored counts two or three,
Whether it be by You or Me,
A Free Throw is Only One,
But many a Game, It has Won.

A Lively Game on the Move,
Nothing Prettier than in the Groove,
The Whole Team Being in a Zone,
To Claim a Victory of Their Own.

BOWLING

A Rolling Sport with a ball.
Release carefully; do not fall.
Wipe the ball with your towel.
Make sure you do not foul.
Get many pins with a throw.
Knock 'em down all in a row.
At least try for the spare.
Add it to the scoring square.
Better yet, shoot for strikes.
Is what everyone really likes.
Post it Proudly with Your Name.
Knowing You Found Your Bowling Game.

FOOTBALL

Kickoffs for games start and after each score,
As your team endeavors for more.
On returns advance as far as you can,
As you execute this phase of the plan.

Block, Tackle, Pursue and Hit,
Run formations that try to fit,
The right defense on each play,
Or the right offense to go all the way.

Secure the ball, hold it tight,
Give your all with exerted might,
On defense plug the hole, stop the run,
Defend the pass 'til the game is won.

Offensive schemes by both teams,
To create holes in the seams.
Whether by run or the pass,
The winning score you try to amass.

When offenses are stymied punt the ball.
Turn it over to the defensive call,
To hold firm with positioned ground,
On your opponent continue to hound.

Should you lose, don't feel bad.
As long as you gave all you had.
Hopefully when the game is done.
Your team will have a victory won.

BIKE RIDES

I have two bikes that I ride.
One Inside, One Outside.
The Inside One is an Aerdyne.
Titled with name as mine.
While riding, I sit and count
On the cycle I did mount.
The chance of Watching TV
To Relax and Entertain Me.
20 Minutes to a half an hour.
I move the handle, pull for power.
When time has elapsed.
And it's time to quit.
It's no longer time,
On the bike to sit.

I love to go for a bike ride.
When I can outside.
To travel through community places.
And catch expressions on people's faces.
Breathe in the Earthly Air.
Observing sights everywhere.
Ol' Mother Nature at my door.
Bringing its Seasonal Encore.
The fluid movement of legs and eyes.
Gives my body needed exercise.
When it comes to the final call.
I maneuver to give it my all.
Many reasons to ride my bike.

GOLF

Hit the ball off the mounted tee,
Try to score with a birdie,
Swing the hips with a partial pivot,
Strike solidly, don't leave a divot.
A straight line is shortest to the hole,
In golf is always the treasured goal,
Strike the ball squarely, hit it far,
Try and make at least a par.
Each course has its legal grounds,
Be sure and keep the ball inbounds.
Know very well the lay of the land,
Hit in the fairways and not the sand,
Different clubs, for different folks,
All to minimize the number of strokes.
From driver, to irons, or the wedge,
You try and secure a winning edge.
On the green and over the putter,
The crowd is silent, nary an utter,
To the average player, my hat I doff,
As you try and master the game of golf.

SWIMMING

Whether it be a she or him,
A water sport called Swim,
Involves many practice hours,
To be strong, sleek and trim.

A gun or horn begins the start,
Give all with your soul and heart,
Be it an individual or relay,
Perform with a swimmer's smart.

Breaststroke/Backstroke or the crawl,
Whatever method give your all,
For yourself and your school,
Stand proudly erect and tall.

As you glide through the water,
Whether you be a son or daughter,
Proceed at your maximum pace,
In each highly contested race.

For each watery moment, seize,
The competitive edge with graceful ease.
Be it on front, back or side,
Do it with a winning glide.

Never give up on the notion,
That the water's rippling motion,
Can prevent you from having fun,
Until you're truly Number One.

WRESTLING

After warm-ups, the lights grow dim,
To announce each wrestler's name,
Each match with the spotlight on him.
Engages his foe in the wrestling game.

Weight for weight, pound for pound,
You break down your opponent,
From front and back you come around,
Throughout the battle to prove you own it.

Fast-exerted Action is where it's at,
An individual for himself and team,
Take your foe to the mat,
As your spotlight continues to beam.

Use your savvy, play it wise,
Continue your planned attack,
Shoot for the first place prize,
As you put your competitor on his back.

When in danger, work an escape,
The ultimate goal to win a pin.
With your body fully drape,
To capture that coveted win.

A Half-Nelson/Cradle, whatever hold,
When all is said and done.
Never to your opponent fold,
Come out on top, and be number one.

HOCKEY

Though Hockey is played on ice,
There's such a grace that looks so nice.
With skaters going at full stride,
An ease of action that makes them glide.

Skate with a stick to blast the puck,
Into the opponent's net with skill or luck.
Thrust attack the other team's goal,
Carryout your designated role.

Whether on offense or defense,
Each player must have the skating sense,
To score a goal or a tally,
And when behind, fire a rally.

Over the ice at such a pace,
Sweated forehead and grimace face,
With only one thing in sight,
To score and trigger the On Light.

On Defense protect your Goalie,
The main object being solely,
To stop the offensive thrusts,
Where sticking and checking become musts.

When that final buzzer sounds,
And you've defended your area grounds,
Lineup for post-game handshakes.
Knowing you've given all it takes.

WEIGHT ROOM WONDERS

In the weight room we do many things,
And strenuous effort that it brings.
Many with counted Reps.
One of them is the Steps.
Pushups, running and lifting,
To Our Bodies We are Gifting.
Fitness and strength to Compete,
With Every Opponent We Meet.
Bench Press, Hang Clean, RDL's.
All with Completeness that tells
Us how Our Fitness Efforts Came
To Be embodied in our Name.

SOCCER

Played with a ball so firm and round, in the air and on the ground.
It's mental/physical, all with finesse, to determine which team is
best.

Complete a pass, boot the ball, on the field give your all.
Run overlaps, create open space, get your opponent in a race.
To score in their goal, by giving all your heart and soul.

Use your head, use your feet, on the opponent that you meet,
You should never yield on the Athletic playing field.
The best and hearty will prevail knowing they will not fail,
If they score and execute well, To win and ring the Victory Bell.

TENNIS

A ball, a racquet, and a net,
You serve an ace, fault, or let,
Slow or fast such a pace you'll get,
To try and win each battled set.

Play with skill and nerves so loose,
Until the game reaches deuce,
Get your opponent out of sync,
With that short lob called a dink.

Backhand, forehand, hit with power,
Standout and shine like a sturdy flower,
If you successfully do all the above,
Then Tennis truly is a game of Love.

VOLLEYBALL

On offense, serve the ball over the net,
On defense, receive and forward set,
To spike the ball for a kill,
With all your might and determined will.

How many times can you come up big?
On the return, when you dive and dig,
To earn needed points for your team,
With a planned attack and scheme.

When making an airborne serve,
Do it with resolving nerve,
Keep the ball inbounds,
With maximum effort, and grunted sounds.

Of Defense, solid as a rock,
At the net attempt to block,
Your team winning the ball,
With the ump's favorable call.

Never give up or go in retreat,
Of any opponent that you meet,
Positive attitudes, unity in kin,
As you endeavor for the win.

Regular sets or in Pool Play,
Let your actions pave the way,
And when the matches are done,
Win or lose you're number one.

IOWA SENIOR OLYMPICS

HELLO, from the Iowa Senior Olympic Games.
We Welcome your presence and Your Names.
RAISE THE TORCH, Let the Games Begin.
With All of Our Events that have their spin.

We have entries for everyone's liking,
Bocce Ball, Card Games, even biking.
For an Indoor Game there's Bowling,
Balls down the alley do the rolling.

A Hawkeye Original with a pit,
A thrown Horseshoe to make a hit.
A ball, a net, and maybe a glove,
With Hitting, Lobbing, a game of Love.

We have a pool for those who swim.
Whether it be a she or him.
A softball to hit with the bat,
A Swing, A Hit, Did I do that?

Another ball on the court,
Basketball is a Shooting Sport.
Another game that does belong,
A Ball and a Paddle, Ping-Pong.

Running Events that go with Track,
Regardless of where in the Pack.
Never Stop and Look Back.
Always do the Best You Can.
Don't be known as an Also Ran.

So, whatever is your proven desire.
Do Your Best with Competitive Fire.
Remember the Camaraderie and friends made.
For Lasting Memories Do Not Fade.
Glad YOU Came and were Here.
Hope to see YOU, again Next year.

THE DRAKE RELAYS

Welcome to the famous Drake Relays.
Weathered by cold, wet, and balmy days.
For starters, The Beautiful Bulldog Contest.
With one of them Crowned The Best.
Next is the Annual Colorful Parade.
Viewers watching in the Sun or Shade.
Co-ed Athletes from Colleges, Universities, High Schools.
All competing with their talented Tools.
We are anchored by our Sponsors' Tents.
That make possible all our events.
Quick at the Start, aim for the Wire.
Outpouring of Energy, makes the body tire.
So many events in which to compete.
Old and New Athletes at this Meet.
The Field Events with Exerted Running.
Fans getting their tans of sunning.
Special Events for visiting Pros.
Participating against familiar Foes.
One has to commend the supporting crowd.
With Oral Cheers That Come Out Loud.
The Workers, Judges, all the Staff.
Provide Service to the Relays Graph.
The Stadium will remember the Cheers.
That it embraced over the Years.
Glad you came and were Here.
Hope to See You Again Next Year.

CHEERLEADERS

We are the ones, who lead your cheers,
And need echoing responses for our ears.
If the crowd doesn't follow, It's hard to lead,
We need Your Chorus on which to feed.

We don't brag, we don't boast,
We always give our exerted most.
Come join us as we lead the way,
For all Our Teams when they play.

We practice hard in hours long,
To do the cheers and School Song.
Students and fans need to know,
We need your support to do our show.

We Strongly believe in what we do,
And our audience should truly too.
We represent our Community as well as School,
Accepted Warmth Can Be Oh So Cool!

We Perform with Youthful Soul,
Being the Best is Our Cherished Goal.
So each time YOU Attend a Game,
Remember We're more than just a Name.

When all is over and said and done,
We want Our Teams to be NUMBER ONE.
And Show Our Competitors We CAN,
BE OUR TEAM'S UNITED FAN!

Academics

HISTORY

It repeats itself, a Truth or Mystery?
This subject known as History.
All the dates, times and places,
Different cultures, religions, races;
Watery fountains, snowcapped mountains,
Grassy meadowlands, deserts' arid sands,
If we counted all earthly spaces,
All of the people and their faces;
We'd capture a special moment of time,
When those eras reached their prime.
On this Terra Firma called earth,
We trace all from their birth,
Through good times and bad with stress,
In some instances under duress,
During peacetime as well as wars,
Heredity passed on, opened doors.
To improve the world for all to see,
All filtered down to you and me.
To give us all some kind of sense,
To understand the recorded events.

ACCOUNTING

In Accounting, when one looks.
At a particular set of books.
All entries to an account.
Documented by a dollar amount.
For Liabilities and Assets.
That denote all facets
Of a Credit or Debit,
A Plus or a Minus.
An Increase or Decrease.
That properly define us.
A Statement of Income Flow.
Where the dollars come and go.
Hopefully each named Asset.
Will cover an Expense Offset.
An Accounting or Calendar Year.
All the information is shown here.
Hoping to show a positive sign.
To improve that Bottom Line.

PERFORMING ARTS

Drama, Speech, and Acting.
With Live Audiences Reacting,
To Music and the Spoken Word.
To be Seen as Well as Heard.

Choirs with their melodies to sing,
Such vocalization they can bring.
Expressive Actions come with song
Showing together they belong.

Memorization of words and lines.
All done with tell-tale signs.
To characterize coveted roles.
Outpouring of Hearts and Souls.

Receptive audiences to listen and hear.
To enjoy the actions and to cheer.
Be it Music or a Storied Theme.
Performed by Individuals or a Team.

E.L.P.

Here I sit in E.L.P.,
Wondering at what I see.
Each student is oh so smart,
With all the things they do impart.

Yet, they're so normal acting,
Their actions aren't retracting.
Confident/Relaxed, lots of poise,
Occasional outbursts of fun filled noise.

The inward working of the brain,
Promote results of endless drain.
On subject matters so broad and deep,
On solo efforts for them to keep.

Academic Decathlon, or Mock Trial,
Events that allow them to compile
Facts and Figures for competition,
The correct answers to completion.

Through it all such composure,
Giving all some kind of closure.
Moving from High School to College,
To learn and expand newfound knowledge.

SPEECH

Get In The Mood.
Don't Be Rude.
Choose Your Style.
Accent A Smile.
Be Aware of Feelings.
In Your Open Dealings.
Body Language Try and Mirror.
To Your Audience as Your Hearer.
CHARISMA, Connecting with the Crowd.
In Toneful Voices Soft and Loud.
We All Have It To Some Degree.
Displaying Ourselves For All To See.

HEALTH

What can one say to their Health?
It's not about Money or Wealth.
But Physical Conditions of Body and Mind.
All the things that Affect it in Kind.

The bones, the lungs, and the heart.
Is where one could easily start.
Of Earthly things affecting them all.
Whether they be Big or Small.

Proper Diet will help them endure.
To prevent ailments and possible cure.
Along with Meaningful Exercise.
To Keep the Body Healthy and Wise.

The Circulating System and its Flow.
Helps with Navigation To and Fro.
Whether it's Resting or on the Go.
Its Total Workings One Should Know.

Make sure that with Proper Care.
That the Body doesn't Dare.
To Breathe in a Deadly Air.
So its Functions will Properly Fare.

It's Important to Make Right Choices.
In the Mind You'll Hear the Voices.
So STOP and LISTEN, DON'T SMOKE OR DRINK.
YOU'LL BECOME WHAT YOU DO AND THINK!!!

ARTS

Art depicts and comes from many things,
And the endless joy that it brings.

There is acting, there is writing,
Both can be so inviting.
Acting with its outspoken word,
Writing within that can't be heard.

There is music played as well as singing,
Its enjoyment can be so ringing,
To the inward soul and listening ear,
To those who understand and hear.

We have paintings and drawings, songs and plays,
Art can be expressed in so many ways,
Pictures with texture so fine,
Completed pictorial and colored design.

Done by pencil, computer, and pen,
Authored by women as well as men,
Some are tepid, some are bolder,
Beauty always in the eye of the beholder.

The written plays, the recorded song,
The painted pictures all belong,
What are these things called the Arts?
All of the above that warm the hearts!

HIGH SCHOOL INDUSTRIAL TECH

Industrial Tech, an interesting class.
Be it for a Lad or Lass.
Measurements, rulers, lines to draw.
Machine usage like a power saw.
Outlining, Planning, something to build.
Completed Projects hopefully fulfilled.
Using an assortment of different tools.
Abiding by all the Safety Rules.
Use of Clamps, paints and stains.
To coincide with different grains.
A drill to insert a screw.
Along with some sticking glue.
Paper and nails, use of wood.
To Prove to Yourself you could
Finish your selection to a T.
For classmates and teacher to see.

PHYSICAL EDUCATION (P.E.)

Here I am doing Phys. Ed.,
Some kids like, some just dread.
We have volleyball and swim,
For both a she and a him.
Along with paddle ball and Ping-Pong,
To make the reflexes quick and strong,
Physical Fitness — all kinds of machines,
To grow young bodies' inherited genes.
Walking, Hiking and mile running,
Roller blading, and Tennis sunning.
Even time for silent reading,
A pause from the physical bleeding.
All to grow the body and mind,
To develop each student regardless of kind.

LANGUAGE ARTS

In Language Arts you read and write,
To try and gain some insight,
As to what the author says,
To interpret their writing ways.

Sentence structure of verbs and nouns,
Adjectives, Adverbs, commas, pronouns,
The Meaning and Spelling, use of a Word,
A Telling Story for Readers to be Heard.

Universal Language for All to Be Spoken,
A Special Dialect that can't be Broken,
Such Diligence in the Way One can Write,
Sadness, Tragedy, Joy and Delight.

SCIENCE

Just how much reliance can we put on the Word Science?
Whether Actuarial or Physical, Is it known or just Mystical?
How Do the birds Fly in the Sky?
Does the Sun Come Up or Go Down, Or Does It Just Rotate Around?

Why is there Darkness/Daylight, Bright in the Day, Starry at Night?
Chemical Reactions Taking Place, Affecting the Whole Human Race,
Documentation versus Questioned Defiance, Gives us Our Daily World Science!

TRIBUTE TO OUR ALMA MATER

Here's to You Parsons College.
For furnishing us Academic Knowledge.
You did it successfully for 98 years.
Tho' it ended in Heartbreak and Tears.
However, Your Memory lingers on.
Although, you are physically gone.
Reincarnated in a different phase.
Doesn't Alter the Memorable Ways,
Your Guidance was directed at Each Student.
In a Manner that Proved Most Prudent.
To Help Each Person Navigate Life.
To Succeed and Conquer Strife.
We Remember the Hallowed Halls.
And Memories that Echoed from the Walls.
That Invigorated Our Most Inner Soul.
To Live and Play Our Earthly Role.
Although, We Are All Born Into Birth.
Eventually, Our Bodies Will Depart This Earth.
Regardless of Where We Finally Go.
Your Guiding Light Will Always Glow!!!

PARSONS COLLEGE SPIRIT

Here we gather in 2004,
Old acquaintances to renew once more,
These last 50 years really flew,
A Big Warm Welcome to Each of You.

Though our school is officially gone,
Its lasting memories linger on,
Barhydt Chapel, Parsons Hall,
The Homecoming Dance, The Winter Ball,
Freshmen Beanies in the fall.

The Sororities and our Frat,
We knew where the action was at.
Most importantly, friendship of a brother,
To support and encourage one another.

Our Parsons training bode us well,
We're not afraid to Shout and Yell,
Our bodies reflect a immense pride,
With many memories endeared inside.

Stop and smell the roses, What an appropriate phrase,
For all of us in our retirement days.
Stop/Look/Listen, I'm sure you'll hear it,
That reborn again Parsons Spirit.

OUR DEMOCRATIC GOVERNMENT

Our Government entails many People and Laws.
And throughout history had some flaws.
Through Our System there were Corrections.
To try and find the right Connections.
From Executive, Legislative and Judicial.
Amendments and Bills, all so Crucial.
For the benefit of the Masses.
Ethnic Groups of Different Classes.
The President in Authoritative Action.
Provides only a Small Fraction.
Of the Work and Overall Process.
Congress is Challenged to do the rest.
Their Efforts should always be the best.
To do what is Right for All Concerned.
With Many Lessons to be Learned.
The Treasury, Civil Liberties, Passage of Laws.
All meant for the Rightful Cause.
Economics and the Courts come into play.
To move the Country in the Right Way.
Time will tell if Democracy will Last.
Or join Failed Civilizations of the Past.

GEOGRAPHY

We live in a World, Also called Earth.
With living things coming from Birth.
Plants with Photosynthesis, Animals around.
Reaching for air, as well as the ground.
Mountains, Rivers, Deserts, Trees.
Warm Temperatures, and Colds that freeze.
Multiple Atmospheres, Ultra-Violet Rays.
Darkness at Nights, Sunlight for the Days.
Cyclones, Tornadoes, Strong Monsoons.
Different components, along with Moons.
People, Culture, Religion, Races.
Skin Colors reflected in the Faces.
An Atlas will include Topography.
All are Embodied in our Geography.

SUBSTITUTE TEACHING

Why do I substitute Teach?
It's the students I try to reach.
Each having a special trait.
On Which the teacher can rate.
Hopefully they will do their best.
To master a subject and classroom test.
To prepare them for life's quest.
For success on which to rest.
A journey that will be hard and long.
To prevail they must be strong.
Doing the right and not the wrong.
Reaching a plateau they can inspire.
To attain goals and reach much higher.

POETRY MONTH

It's Poetry Month with Written Prose.
To Entertain and Brighten Those
Who Feel the Meaning of Each Word.
To Make the Verses Understood.
Descriptive Language to Present.
To Those Readers Who Consent.
And the Material it Contains.
It's Thoughts in Mind That Remains.

Seasons
&
Holidays

SPRING

Plant the garden with things to sow,
Keep out the weeds with garden hoe,
Up in the air is a flowing sight,
A tail flying precisioned kite.

Spring has sprung; the grass is green,
Everywhere one looks is a beautiful scene.
The leaves are out on the trees,
Blooming flowers attract the bees.

Birds pair off and build a nest,
Species survival belongs to the best.
Squirrels are busy gathering food,
Eating, burying, whatever the mood.

Insects, mosquitoes, bugs, and flies,
Come in droves as no surprise.
The clippers come out, motors are going,
Especially those to do the mowing.

Wash the windows, clean the yard,
Springtime work can be very hard,
On unused muscles out of tone,
Working themselves to the very bone.

Enjoy it all, it doesn't last,
Capture the season and its cast.
Summer comes soon with its heated blast,
And Spring becomes a thing of the past.

SPRINGTIME

The rain is falling.
The birds are calling.
Springtime is on the mend.
Culminating Winter's end.

Leaves will come to foil.
As people begin to toil.
Grass will turn to green.
Blooming flowers are a scene.

Everything begins to thrive.
Bushes/Trees come alive.
Aromatic odors fill the air.
Outward actions begin to flare.

Rolling clouds in the sky.
Floating particles pass by.
All come available to bring.
This season known as Spring.

SUMMERTIME

With the growing season about to resume,
Summertime is now in full bloom.
Wet summer rains come and go,
Making us forget the winter snow.
Boating, swimming and lots of running,
Heated weather with tans of sunning.
Gardens produce their many kinds,
Outdoor exploring with its finds.
Yards to mow, things to grow,
Summer breezes on the blow.
Rich green yards and many flowers,
All enriched by summer showers.
Hurried activity by birds and bees,
With full foliage on the trees,
To hide squirrels and the birds,
Seeking neighbors have kind words.
Enjoy the beauty of it all,
For soon to follow comes the fall.

FALL

Fall is coming so very soon,
To play its own melodic tune.
With Wind, Rain and falling leaves,
To clog each house's hanging eaves.

The ducks and geese southward head,
And a human cleans out a flowerbed,
To complete a cycle with windy swirl,
Last minute work for each tiny squirrel.

The Color and Sights of Splendor,
For people's eyes to See and Render,
Such Annual Beauty that does abound,
With Leaves cascading to the ground.

Picturesque colors of Bushes and Trees,
Late Blooming Flowers to attract the bees,
Such Hustle and Bustle by all concerned,
To ready themselves for winter's turn.

WINTER

Winter has arrived, the winds are blowing,
The skies are graying, soon to be snowing.
The Wind Index and the Winter Chill,
Definitely affect the Utility Bill.
When the sun is shining, the snow is bright,
Creating a Wonderland also at night.
There's skiing and sledding, snowmen to build,
Fireplaces are burning with tummies to be filled.
Icicles hang from the eaves and the trees,
One can hear an occasional sneeze.
There are so many items Winter can bring,
All fade away as we head into spring.

HOLIDAYS

VALENTINE'S DAY

This is the Day for all the Hearts,
Where True Affection always starts,
To the Ones we're Thinking of,
Pledging our Lasting Steadfast Love.

PRESIDENTS DAY

This is National Presidents Day.
To Honor Those Who Paved the Way.
First, Our Founder Who Gave Direction.
Another Made a Distinctive Correction.
About our Country's Moral Code.
Where to Head Down the Road.
A Complex Process of Changing Hearts.
Where True Healing Always Starts.
With Repair Work Still To Be Done.
To Keep Our Nation Number One.
We Also Honor the Many Others.
For Their Service as Duties Brothers.

ST. PATRICK'S DAY

As we celebrate St. Patrick's Day
The likes of which we've never seen,
Leprechauns will lead the way
And the wearing of the Green.
There'll be boasting and toasting,
With Lots and Lots of Green beer,
Along with Corned Beef and Cabbage,
And Irish songs to hear.

EASTER

It's Easter Time with Lent and Fasting,
To Honor our Savior Everlasting,
Count your Blessings and Your Prayers,
To a Higher Power Who Really Cares.

MOTHER'S DAY

Today we revere all the Mothers,
From Siblings, Sisters and Brothers,
To those of you both Present and Past.
Thanks for memories that forever last.

MEMORIAL DAY

As we approach this Memorial Day,
Have Hope, Give Thanks, and Pray;
That all our wars are in the past,
And PEACE will forever last.

FLAG DAY

Today we Honor our country's flag,
As Americans we're proud to brag,
Of things we Say and our actions too,
Color Us All, RED, WHITE and BLUE.

FATHER'S DAY

Your Patience/Guidance led my way,
Molding the Person I Am Today.
Thanks for your confidence in me,
Shaping my being for the World To See.

FOURTH OF JULY

As we celebrate each Fourth of July,
And watch our Flag so proudly fly;
Give thanks to those who kept us free,
Preserving for us our Liberty.

URBANDALE, IOWA'S 4TH OF JULY CELEBRATION

We are the 4th of July Committee.
When we pay Tribute to our City.
Providing this Annual Celebration.
Makes it One of the Best in the Nation.
There's a Carnival, rides and games.
With their signs and identifying names.
The Merry-Go-Round, the Tilt-A-Whirl.
Providing fun for a Boy or Girl.
The Midway has Vendors that Sell.
Various Foods with an Aromatic Smell.
Be it a Sandwich or Ice Cream.
Served individually or by a team.
Lions Club Bingo Tent and its Winners.
Available to any player, even Beginners.
Music is provided by various Bands.
With Silent Listeners, or Clapping Hands.
Merchants donate Prizes to Win.
If you Hold the Winning Pin.
There's a Bike Ride, Races to Run.
All providing Athletic Fun.
We cooperate with the city Police.
Another part of the event to piece.
Along with a Colorful Car Show.
Varied models can go Fast or Slow.
Most important is the entrant Parade.
With viewers in the Sun or the Shade.
Fireworks are provided by Buttons Sold.
Its Visual Display is a Sight to Behold.
So in Conclusion, Again Next Year.
This Committee will Reappear.

LABOR DAY

We honor our workers on this day,
Whose Sweat and Toil Paved the way,
Improving our lives while here on earth,
Advancing each generation's Total Worth.

HALLOWEEN

Here it is Halloween,
With Witches, Goblins, Ghosts.
Sights that are Yearly Seen,
And Black Cats Climbing Posts.

Although it is Dark and Scary,
Costumed Children seem to enjoy,
With their Buckets to carry,
Treats for a Girl or Boy.

The Moonlight Sky provides some light,
For Tricksters to find their way,
Providing a Spectacular Sight,
To End This Spooky Day.

VETERANS DAY I

Your Sense of Duty on What To Do,
For Our Country's Red, White and Blue.
We're greatly indebted and will always be,
For Protecting our Cherished Liberty.

VETERANS DAY II

So Glad YOU were on Our Side,
Those still Living and Those Who Died.
Your sense of Duty, as well as Pride,
Engrained so Deeply Down Inside.

VETERANS DAY III

November 11 is Veterans Day,
To Honor Those Who Paved the Way,
THEIR SACRIFICES should never be Lost,
With MANY LIVES WARS Have Cost,
So FLY THE FLAG, JOIN THE PARADE,
BE Proud to BRAG, for FREEDOM MADE,
Listen to the STAR-SPANGLED BANNER,
Let ALL Display the Proper Manner,
REMOVE THE HATS, HANDS OVER HEARTS,
A TRUE PATRIOT Is Where It Starts.

THANKSGIVING

Isn't it great, just to be living!
As we approach this Thanksgiving.
Enjoy the turkey, and its dressings,
Be Thankful for all Your Blessings!

CHRISTMAS

As we approach this Holiday Season,
Is there any Rhyme or Reason?
Why the Goodwill, Shouldn't Abound,
To and Through Us the Whole Year Round?

YULETIDE FEELINGS/THOUGHTS

Here's to you during this Holiday Season,
With its Pretty Sights, and People Sneezin';
All the Goodies, and Aromatic Smells,
Sated Taste buds, as the Appetite Swells;
The Tummy expands, and then it adjusts
Too all the Intakes that become musts.
Melodic Music fills the Wintry Air,
As People's Feelings show they care;
In Action/Words, linked Like-kind,
Harmony/Unison aren't hard to find;
Yuletide Greetings especially to you,
In All You Say and All You Do!
Stop, Look, Listen, Inhale it all,
Enjoy a Festive Free Holiday Ball!

NEW YEARS

Have a Cool Yule, and a Cheer Year!
Toast each other with Wine and Beer!
Everything will be just fine,
If we sing Auld Lang Syne!

Patriotism

WHAT AMERICA MEANS TO ME

The clothes that I wear, the right of Piety,
The people I meet everywhere, that's America to Me.
The Businesses, the Shoppers, all working in Harmony,
The Butcher and the Farmer, that's America to Me.
All the thoughts I possess within, the Right to be Brave and Free,
The House I live in, that's America to Me.

The right to an Education, To explain My Beliefs and Me,
Striving to better my Nation, that's America to Me.
The Plains and the Valleys, Rivers flowing to the sea,
The Trees, Streets, and Alleys, that's America to Me.

The Fathers and the Mothers, The Flag Waiving so Free,
The Sisters and the Brothers, that's America to Me.
The Beautiful Towns and Cities, that Shine so Splendidly,
Poets with their enchanting ditties, that's America to Me.

The Sky high above, that flows to Eternity,
The People that I love, that's America to Me.
Transportation and Travel, All of Nature's Beauty,
These all unravel America to Me.

Opportunities lie before me, If only I could see,
Sing Loudly with the Chorus, America is for me.
I could write forever as one can plainly see,
I'll give my best endeavor, America's for me.

KOREAN/VIETNAM HONOR FLIGHT

To you Veterans of Your War.
YOU DID WHAT OUR FLAG STANDS FOR.
Serving Your Country Notably.
Preserving Our Precious Liberty.
Side by Side for One Another.
Camaraderie Made YOU A BROTHER.
To Battle a Dreaded Foe.
Hitting them Blow after Blow.
A PILOT, SEAMAN, SOLDIER, MARINE.
All were thrust into a Horrible Scene.
Our THANK YOUS, Should Never End.
For Your RESOLVE Did Never Bend.
So HONOR YOURSELF and the Day.
And ACCOLADES that come YOUR WAY.
YOU Answered our Country's Call.
YOU SERVED, GIVING YOUR ALL.
In the Parades That Come Marching By.
First Thing To Catch The Searching Eye.
Is OLD GLORY LEADING THE WAY.
REFLECTING OUR FREEDOM, WE HAVE TODAY.

OUR FLAG — OLD GLORY

Waving in the wind, flies OLD GLORY,
Her evolvement is quite a story.
Progressing through her various stages.
Enduring so much through all the ages.

From the British-American War,
The Birth of Freedom she originally bore,
Through tattered times from a beginner,
She's proved our nation is a winner.

The Civil War was about slavery,
And battles fought with such bravery,
To unite our Country in a common cause,
To work out our diversity flaws.

Spanish American, World War One.
Gave temporary peace when said and done.
The Big War was World War II,
To bring lasting peace to Me and You.

In 2001 there was a terrorist attack,
To try and set our nation back,
The will of our people is faithful and strong.
We will prove the terrorists WRONG!!!

In parades that come marching by,
First thing to catch the searching eye.
Is OLD GLORY leading the way.
Reflecting our freedom we have today.

HONOR FLIGHTS

To all you Veterans of WWII.
This Flight is to HONOR YOU!!!
For Serving Your Country Notably.
Preserving Our Precious Liberty.
Side by side for One Another.
Your Camaraderie Made YOU A BROTHER.
To Defeat Two Dreaded Foes.
Dealing Them Their Final Blows.
Your Memorial is now a Hallowed Wall.
So That Each of You Can STAND SO TALL.
A PILOT, SEAMAN, SOLDIER, or MARINE.
All were thrust into a Horrible Scene.
To DEFEAT EVIL, Keep the World Free.
With A Hard Earned Victory.
Our THANK YOUS, Should Never End.
For Your Resolve did never bend.
So HONOR YOURSELF and the Day.
And Accolades that come YOUR WAY.
YOU Answered our Country's Call.
You SERVED GIVING YOUR ALL.
YOU DID WHAT OUR FLAG STANDS FOR.
In the Parades That Come Marching By.
First Thing to Catch the Searching Eye.
Is OLD GLORY Leading the Way.
REFLECTING OUR FREEDOM, WE HAVE TODAY.

STATUE OF LIBERTY

Proudly she stands in all her glory,
Her history tells us quite a story,
An immigrant herself, coming from France,
Giving Freedom a Worthy Chance.

Arm extended and Torch so high,
Her statuesque figure graces the sky,
Exuding Confidence for the World to see,
A Birthmark for us and our posterity.

Erectly she stands with bodice so tall,
She answered our nation's beckon call,
To represent us each and every day,
And to all those who pass her way.

We have our Flag and National Songs,
To energize the Patriotism of our throngs,
Strong in Character, Protector of the Weak,
Her silent presence lets her speak.

Through the years, she's remained so proud,
Standing out in the New York crowd,
When thinking of Freedom and our country's plight,
Remember the LADY — OUR GUIDING LIGHT!!!

SELF AND COUNTRY PRIDE

We Iowans do stand united,
Although we weren't formally invited,
My wife, grandson and I stood in line,
To form a human U.S. flag design

To let terrorists know we're not afraid,
We are True Americans made.
With Spirit, Mind, Heart and Soul,
Each represents a cherished goal,
We are Vibrant, We are Strong,
As we Echo Our Country's Song.

America The Beautiful, Land of the Free,
For All the World to Hear and See,
God Bless America, The Star-Spangled Banner.
Are reflected in our Dignified Manner.

To All the World Terrorists, you can Run and Hide,
You'll never Destroy our Personal or Country's Pride,
That's in Our Hearts, Deep, Down Inside,
In our souls, Patriotism will always reside.

STARS AND STRIPES

Our flag represents our ideals, people, and land.
May it always, proudly, steadfastly stand.

Courage and Hardiness, represent the Red.
With Dignity, and Valor for the Honored dead,
Innocence and Purity stand for the White.
With Charity, Hope, and Eternal Light.
Perseverance and Justice is for the Blue,
Along with Vigilance in all that we do.
Each Individual Star depicts a State.
The 50 in UNISON make our Country Great.
Anytime our Nation has been put to the test,
It always brings out our people's best.

THE PROTECTORS

To the Brothers and Sisters in Blue
Firefighters in Red and Medics, Too
Sense of Duty Always Comes Through
Our Thanks and Praises Go Out To You
When Tragedy Strikes With its Pain
Your Faith and Resolve Surfaces Again
Loyalty, Passion, Comfort, Caring
Bravery, Faith, Support and Sharing
All Embodied in Your Souls
Carrying out Your Duted Roles
You are Peacemakers, Children of God
The Salt of the Earth, on Which We Trod

Observations

OBSERVATIONS

Money

Isn't it so funny,
How people crave money?
And when it's cloudy,
They want it sunny!
As for the little bee,
Sometimes we hardly see,
It's the ONE that makes the HONEY!

Birds

Up above and in the sky,
Different birds flitter and fly,
Chirping sounds can be heard,
Regardless of the type of bird,
When it comes to the final call,
The Dove Of Peace heads them all!

Squirrels

Always working in a whirl,
Is the tiny little squirrel,
No matter how hard they try,
To store their food supply,
Anyway you want it cut,
Their main staple is still the nut!

HELPING HANDS

Strangely enough the folks most apt to lend a hand to you,
Are those already rushed with countless things to do;
Should bad luck befall you and misfortune smack you prone,
The ones who'll help you most of all are those with trouble of
their own.

The folks whose sunny slant on life help heal its smarts and stings,
Are often those who know firsthand the seamy side of things;
He was right, it seems who said, "That life is what you make it,"
It's not always what happens but the way in which you take it.

CIVIL RIGHTS

The 60's had a movement called CIVIL RIGHTS.
A non-violent approach, so there would be no fights.
To end the Demeaning Degradation
That went along with Segregation
Buses carried the Freedom Riders.
They traveled the cause as Insiders.
There was also the Freedom Writers.
Who led with the Pen, non-violent fighters.
The Leader of the Cause was Dr. King.
And the Message he had to bring.
Doing so, with many a Fiery Speech.
To give His Message, and could he Preach!!!
Bombings - Birmingham killed an Innocent Four.
And Our Whole Country Said No More.
So the Negro Nation got their Pact.
On Passing of the Civil Rights Act.

DR. BALL – PRE-OP

I went to Dr. Ball to check my eyes.
And very much to my surprise.
He hit me with cold, hard facts.
I had developed two cataracts.
So, a decision to be made by me.
Decided would do the surgery.
He did the left, then the right.
To help improve my in-sight.
I'll also need new glasses to wear.
I'll keep an old one, as a backup pair.
Thank you doctor for your skills.
Insurance should cover most of the bills.

GRANDKIDS

Oh what a joy, be it girl or boy,
Not of shoulds or dids,
Such a group Grandkids.

They run, skip, and walk,
They scream, holler and talk;
With such energy they expound,
Not a better group can be found.

They with that little wide mouth smile,
Always makes my day worthwhile;
Along with those little sheepish grins,
Is where it all really begins.

To me they never seem to surprise,
With that youthful gleam in their eyes;
All the little things they do impart,
Are always tugging at my heart.

MIRROR REFLECTIONS/QUESTIONS?

I look in the mirror and what do I see?
A reflection of someone, otherwise called me.
And what would happen if the mirror weren't there?

There are two answers:

1. The Vain Answer, "I couldn't stand and stare."
2. The Practical Answer, "I couldn't comb and part my hair."

LIMERICKS

There once was a boy named Flirty,
Who was always getting dirty;
The trouble was,
If he'd used DUZ,
He'd had a Clean Shirty!!!

There once was an Indian named Maisy,
Who nearly drove herself Crazy;
She'd try by the hours,
Attempting to grow flowers,
But all she could raise was a Daisy!!!

There have been many stories told,
Of Pirates' Deeds, both Brave and Bold;
The best by far,
Is they traveled by car
To find a Treasure of Gold!!!

NASCAR

There is a circuit called NASCAR
Which has come from Oh So Far.
Started with bootleggers on the run.
From the Law to get it done.
Drive a vehicle on a track.
Look Ahead - Never Look Back.
A well tuned engine is what you need.
Built for driving and for speed.
Make sure it has plenty of gas.
Either to follow or to pass.
Help is provided by a seasoned crew.
Each member has their job to do.
When you've completed the contested race.
There may be a Big Smile on Your Face.
Something about you can brag.
When you get the checkered flag.

ODDS & ENDS

Seize the Moment, Reap the Treasures,
Work through Torment, Enjoy the Pleasures.

Relatives/Next of Kin, where did it all really begin?
The Garden of Eden, Adam and Eve?
It's Whatever, You Want to Believe!!

This Morn it was Cold and Foggy, The Dew in the Air Made it
Soggy,
As the Fog wore off in the Warming Sun, You Could Almost see it
on the Run.

Knowledge Bowl Testing is Today, Three Teams are entered to
Play,
To do Their Best and try to Advance, To the Finals for One Last
Chance.

The Beautiful Fall Colors on the Trees, Shine Glittering in the
Flowing Breeze,
Close Behind is the Fallout Tease, Soon to Follow, The Colden
Freeze.

WORD RHYME #1

Being Alert, is to be Aware.
Happenings are what One has to Bear.
Consoling Actions show Care.
Risky attempts could be a Dare.
Action/Results is how to Fare.
Bright Sunlight causes Glare.
Most People have some Hair.
A Female Horse is a Mare.
Two of a Kind are a Pair.
Unusual is to be Rare.
An Ogle is a Stare.
A Rip is Also a Tear.
Clothes the Body Can Wear.
I will end this crazy Rhyme.
The Alphabet ran out of Time.

OLD SAGE QUOTES AND MY OWN VERSION

A rolling stone gathers no moss.
(The stone's gain is the moss' loss.)

Early to bed, early to rise, makes a man healthy, wealthy and wise.
(Change man to person, it'll cover the gals and guys.)

It's the early bird that gets the worm.
(If the worm knew that, it might not rise and squirm.)

Still water runs very deep.
(In the ocean of life, does your river seep?)

An apple a day, keeps the doctor away.
(Eat the fruit and save on pay.)

It wasn't that apple in the tree, that did sin to you and me.
(It was that pair on the ground we didn't see.)

Birds of a feather flock together.
(That's how the group endures the weather.)

A penny saved is a penny earned.
(Unless craved, or Inflation burned.)

Jack of all trades, master of none.
(I don't always accomplish, but have lots of fun.)

Out of sight, out of mind.
(If you can't see, you can't find.)

LAW

Sometimes we're all held in awe,
With all the intricacies of the law,
There are numerous kinds of courts,
Those of criminality, those of torts.
There is a Plaintiff and a Defendant,
A Court Bailiff, a Jury to end it,
Overseen by a judge in a robe,
To quote the law and guide the probe.
Rights to Prosecute, Rights to Defend,
To bring a case to its legal end.

PHILOSOPHICAL THOUGHTS

What is One Made Of?
As Life takes its Toll.
Hopefully, Unconditional Love,
And A Strong Inner Soul!

Beauty isn't always seen,
By Humans' Naked eye.
But it can still be keen,
By the Way We Work and Try.

The Clothes that I Wear,
The Color of My Hair,
Bring Nothing to Bear,
Of What I feel and Care!

The Color of One's Skin,
The Words of the Tongue.
Come from Without and Within,
Personalizing a Song to be Sung.

If We Prize the Joys of Life,
And All That It Brings,
Then a man's faithful wife,
Helps heal his Smarts and Stings.

TRAVEL

One way to journey is by boat.
With buoyant water to keep afloat.
For non-drivers take the bus.
Eliminates all the driving fuss.
For time/distance use the plane.
Through the clouds, sun, and rain.
If not motoring very far.
Best use would be the car.
Whether by water, ground or air.
Make sure you arrive safely there.

#2 WORDPLAY

Affirmation is an A-yer,
Purchaser becomes a buyer,
A Chorus can be a Choir,
A Tinter is a Dyer,
Ogling is an Eyer,
A Pilot is a Flyer,
Masculine is a Guyer,
Above is a Little Higher,
Don't get people's Ire,
J is for a J-yer,
K starts a K-yre,
A Fibber is a liar,
What I own is a M-yer,
Evening becomes Nigher,
A Nail for a Plyer,
24 Sheets of Paper is a Quire,
Whiskey has a R-yer,
A Father can be a Sire,
A Car has its Tire,
A Soother is a Unifier,
Music scale has a Ver-nier,
A Telegram is a Wire,
A Nothing Word is Xyre,
A Cowboy is a Yi-ere
A Z-Man is a Zyre.

NEVER STAND ALONE

Stand up for what is right even if standing alone,
Whether it be day or night make your Persona known.

Don't be a loner, fight for what is right,
Maybe it's your choice with verbal spoken voice.
Or actions that may not be heard, doesn't always have to be by
word.
Quite subtle ways can prevail to blow the winds of your sail.

If your efforts lead to humanity's good, then hopefully they'll be
understood,
Your actions won't have been alone; but the final outcome is still
your own.

RAINBOWS

In the sky is a Brilliant Rainbow.
Putting on a Spectacular Show.
Although they develop very slow.
The Final Result is a Vibrant Glow.

They Appear Near the End of a Rain.
The Resulting Outcome is Our Gain.
They Also Depend on the Solar Sun
To Present Colors that Arch Fully Run.

Add the Need for Transparent Light.
To Create This Beautiful Sight.
Tho' They will Eventually Disappear.
From Our Earth's Atmosphere.
We Definitely Know They Were Here.
Surely to Return Again Next Year.

THE TEN COMMANDMENTS

The Ten Commandments aren't MULTIPLE CHOICE!
It's through THE HEART, WE HEAR THE VOICE!!
Always REMEMBER, "THE RULE OF TEN"
LIVE THEM DAILY, AGAIN AND AGAIN!!!!

PLAN AHEAD

It wasn't raining when Noah built his Ark.
His planning didn't leave him in the dark!
With a God Given Talent called FORESIGHT,
He saw the Day and not the Night.
What does this say about ME and YOU?
WE have A Right to this Option too!!!!!

BAD POEM

This Poem is not Good, but Bad,
One Not Happy, but Very Sad.
One not Optimistic, but Depressed,
One not Spoken, but written Expressed.

In Written Words, the Negative Side,
Not In the Open, but to Hide.
The True Meaning of the word Bleak,
In how I write, but Do Not Speak.

To the inwards of my Soul,
Outside the Ring, Not in the Hole.
Allowing Words to Ebb and Flow,
So I must Stop, No More Go.

DIXIE JAZZ BAND MUSIC

Have you ever heard a Dixie Band?
Playing music that is not Canned.
To Audiences that make it FANNED.
To Hear throughout all the Land.
Different instruments being Manned.
With Outpouring Sounds to Understand.
To Patrons that Sit or Stand.
So Many Songs, Where to Begin?
"When The Saints Go Marching In."
Can't forget all the Blues.
From which one can choose.
Livery Stable, Tin Roof, Weary and Farewell.
They have their storied notes to tell.
Another one with Melodious Tones.
Scramble out them "Rattlin' Bones."
This one sounds so Sweet.
The Standard called "Basin Street."
"Jelly Roll Blues," "Tiger Rag,"
"Darktown Strutters' Ball,"
And Who Can't Recall.
"Do You Know What it Means
To Miss New Orleans" and Dixie Queens?
All coming from years in the Past.
This Music has proven it will last.
For it Contains that Dixie Flavor.
For Any Listener who wants to Savor.

QUESTIONS

Tell me why a lighthouse shines?
Or Why a Pine Tree pines.
Also why a canine whines?
Numbers before and after nines.
Why do boats need their oars?
Or Why the Ocean roars.
Why do planes need their wings?
Or the bird as it sings.
Reasoned questions with their answers.
Helps Civilizations understand.
All part of life's enhancers.
Controlled by the Creator's Hand.

L.S.D.

Considering Ideas and points of Views, We have the right to choose, or
reject those of others.
Along with this in our dealings, we verbally or by actions express feelings to
Friends, Sisters, and Brothers.

What You Say, and What You Do, Isn't always my Perception of You!
What I Do, and What I See, Isn't always your Perception of Me!

What about an individual's self-esteem?
Hard-work, Dedication doesn't mean a thing,
You think you're a Player, part of a team,
Doesn't that have a familiar ring???

50 should be the prime of life, but I have to fight to survive;
What do I tell my wife, when it's "out to pasture" at 55?
The word Loyalty in this firm doesn't exist anymore,
The Dollar Sign is the only term they see, as you go out the door!

Hell, I'm not even 52, My Company's telling me I'm through,
What's a Proud Man supposed to do? Get lost from the Company Point-of-
View.
(Retire — Fifty Five Skidoo!!!!)

PILLOW THOUGHTS

As you sleep gently in your bed.
Comfort lies beneath your head.
Sweet Dreams my Child to YOU.
Hopefully they will all come True.
This is for you young Child.
A Cushion so soft and mild.
It will provide a gentle rest.
Through your sleepful quest,
As you sleep in bed tonight.
With comforting dreams that might
Make you rested and when awaken.
Will guide the spirit your mind has taken.
Go to sleep with thoughts so deep.
As you lie in bed, Comfort lies under the Head.
Rest for me So I can see
Comfort to be, Under Me.

Acknowledgments

I am deeply grateful to my family, friends, and students who encourage me in my writing. A special thanks to Margaret Clinkinbeard, my high school teacher, who said that I had the ability to write poetry and gave me the confidence to continue writing throughout my lifetime.